GRAMPA AND JULIE:
SHARK HUNTERS
by jef czekaj
D1308838
HOW I SPENT MY
SUMMER VACATION

Grampa and Julie: Shark Hunters

Published by
Czekaj Press
Box 440422. Somerville, MA 02144-0006
http://www.czekaj.com
e-mail: jef@czekaj.com

Distributed by
Top Shelf Productions
Box 1282. Marietta, GA 30061-1282
http://www.topshelfcomix.com

Much of this book originally appeared in a different form in the pages of *Nickelodeon Magazine*. Pages 18-37 are a redrawn version of a story that appeared in the October, November, December 1999 and January/February 2000 issues. Pages 40-61 originally appeared in the June/July, August, September, October, and November 2000 issues, pages 64-85 originally appeared in the June/July, August, September, October, and November 2001 issues, pages 88-106 originally appeared in the September, October, November 2002, December/January, and February 2003 issues. Throughout the book, the stories have been reformatted, material has been redrawn and edited, and new material has been added. The original strips were edited by Chris Duffy and the staff of *Nickelodeon*. Brett Warnock provided production assistance.

This book was funded in part by a grant from the Xeric Foundation.

Czekaj, Jef
Grampa and Julie: Shark Hunters/ Jef Czekaj
ISBN 1-891830-52-X

First Printing.
Printed in China.

JULIE?
JULIE!
HUH?

JULIE, ARE YOU EVEN **LISTENING** TO HEATH'S REPORT ABOUT WHAT HE DID OVER THE SUMMER?
YES, MS. COOPER.
Eat Your Veggies!
5÷1=X
7×3=47
2 +2 5

HE BEAT HIS BROTHER AT "ROBOT NINJA APOCALYPSE SEVEN" OR SOMETHING.

NO!
YOU'RE TOTALLY WRONG!
NO!

IT'S "ROBOT NINJA APOCALYPSE **SIX**"! **SIX**!
SIX, MS. COOPER!
IT'S OKAY, HEATH. REALLY.

JULIE, DO YOU HAVE YOUR REPORT PREPARED?

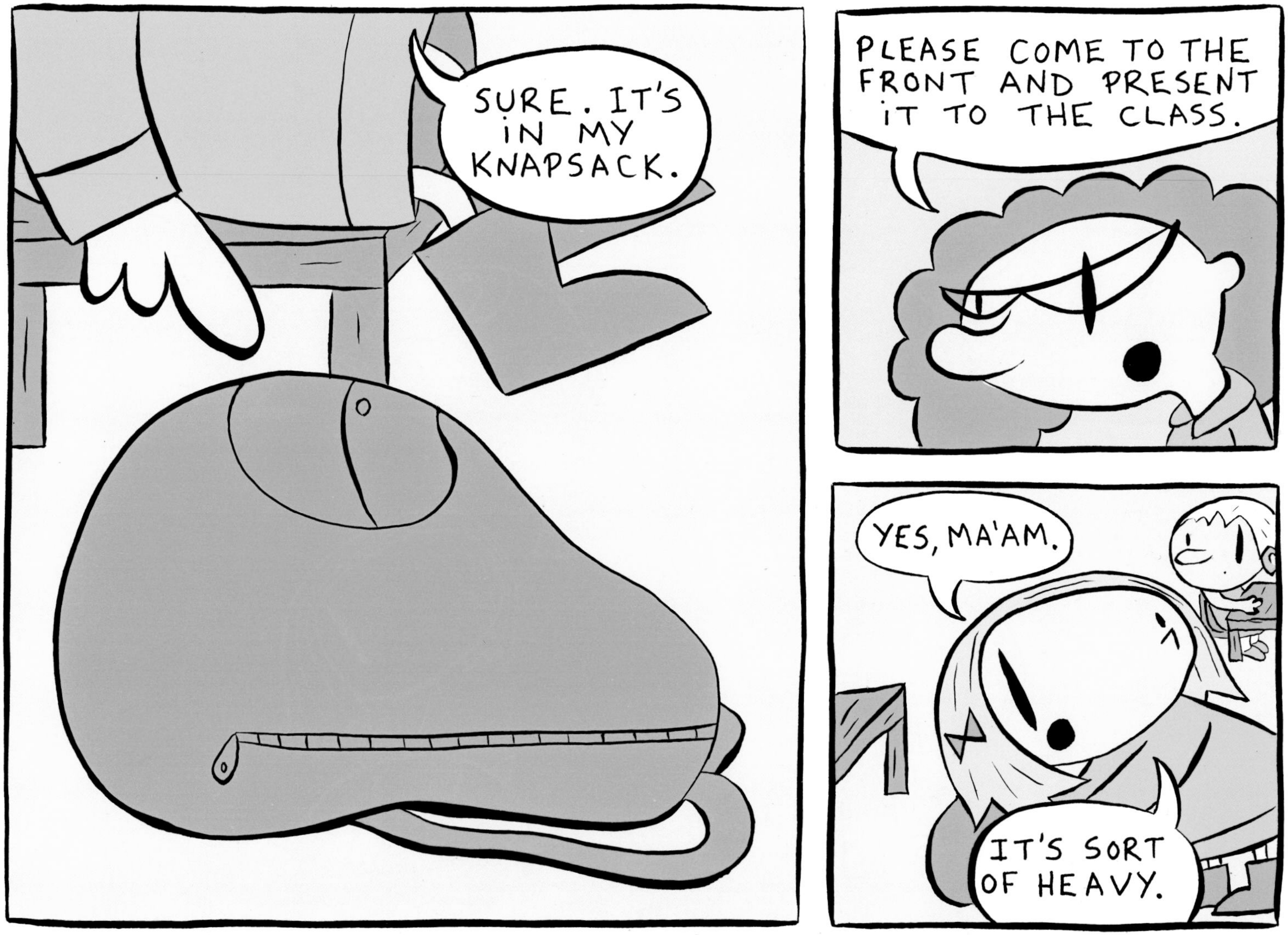

SURE. IT'S IN MY KNAPSACK.

GRRR
MNMMN
TAP
TAP
♫

HiYAH!
MMNRGM
GNSRRGHH

PANT
PANT

ZZZZIP!

Aa Bb Cc Dd Ee Ff
Gg Hh Ii Jj Kk Ll
Mm Nn Oo Pp Qq etc.
!
?
ZZZ

UNZIP
RUSTLE
RUSTLE
GRUNT
My Summer Vacation
GRRR
HMMF
My Summer Vacation

MMMMFF
My Summer Vacation

AAHHHH!
My Summer Vacation

OOOOF!
SLAM

WHEW

IT'S KIND OF A LONG STORY.
My Summer Vacation

"WHAT I DID ON MY SUMMER VACATION, BY JULIE"
CHAPTER ONE

OUR ART
YAWN
Z Z
BLAB
BLAB
Z Z
PICK
SCRATCH
WHISPER
COMICS
FILE
BLIP
BLIP
TEEN NEW YORKER
UM, UH.

"GRAMPA AND I WERE SOMEWHERE IN THE ATLANTIC OCEAN..."
Z Z Z

chapter one

GRAMPA AND I WERE SOMEWHERE IN THE ATLANTIC OCEAN ON A SCIENTIFIC QUEST TO FIND STEPHEN, THE LARGEST SHARK IN THE WORLD.

SHIVER ME TIMBERS!
YO HO HO AND A BOTTLE OF RUM!

BLOW THE MAN, DOW-OH, HEH-HEH, HI, JULIE, I DIDN'T SEE YOU THERE.
TAP
TAP

GRAMPA, YOU'RE NOT PRETENDING YOU'RE A PIRATE AGAIN, ARE YOU?

OH, AND BY THE WAY, HAVE YOU SEEN OUR MAP?
UM...

NOPE, SURE HAVEN'T SEEN IT, NO WAY.

QUIT FOOLING AROUND! EVERYONE KNOWS YOU'RE A FAMOUS FISH SCIENTIST ON AN IMPORTANT MISSION TO FIND AND STUDY STEPHEN THE SHARK.
FIGURE ONE
STEPHEN
GRAMPA
I KNOW, I KNOW...

I JUST THINK IT WOULD BE MORE GLAMOROUS TO BE A PIRATE: GOLD DOUBLOONS, PARROTS ON SHOULDERS, SCURVY, ALL THAT FUN STUFF.

PEQUOD

DO YOU SEE ANYTHING INTERESTING IN THE TELESCOPE?

SOON...
...AND WHEN WE SAW STEPHEN THE SHARK WE GOT SO SCARED THAT WE CRASHED OUR PLANE INTO THE OCEAN.
RAP
WHERE WERE YOU GOING?

WE WERE ON OUR WAY TO THE WORLD RAPPING CHAMPIONSHIP.
RAP
YEAH, LAST YEAR WE WON AN AWARD!

WOW, THAT'S SUPER!
WORST RAPPERS
DJ CHICKEN
MC SQUIRREL
UH, NOT EXACTLY.

WANT TO HEAR A SONG? WE'VE BEEN PRACTICING.
WELL, ACTUALLY, WHY DON'T YOU TELL US **EXACTLY** WHERE YOU LAST SAW STEPHEN THE SHAR–

BOOM
RAP
BOOM
WICKA WICKA

(RAPPING)
WELL MY NAME IS MC SQUIRREL, MY FAVORITE COLOR IS ORANGE, AND I'VE GOT MORE RHYMES THAN, UH, UM, UH, WELL LET'S SEE...

BOOM

SCRATCH

RAP

MAP

SKIP

BOOM

BOOM

ARRGH!

UM, GRAMPA, YOU CAN STOP DANCING NOW. THE SO-CALLED "MUSIC" HAS STOPPED.
NO, I CAN'T. THE BEAT'S IN MY...

FEEE-
SLIP

EET!
KERSPLASH!

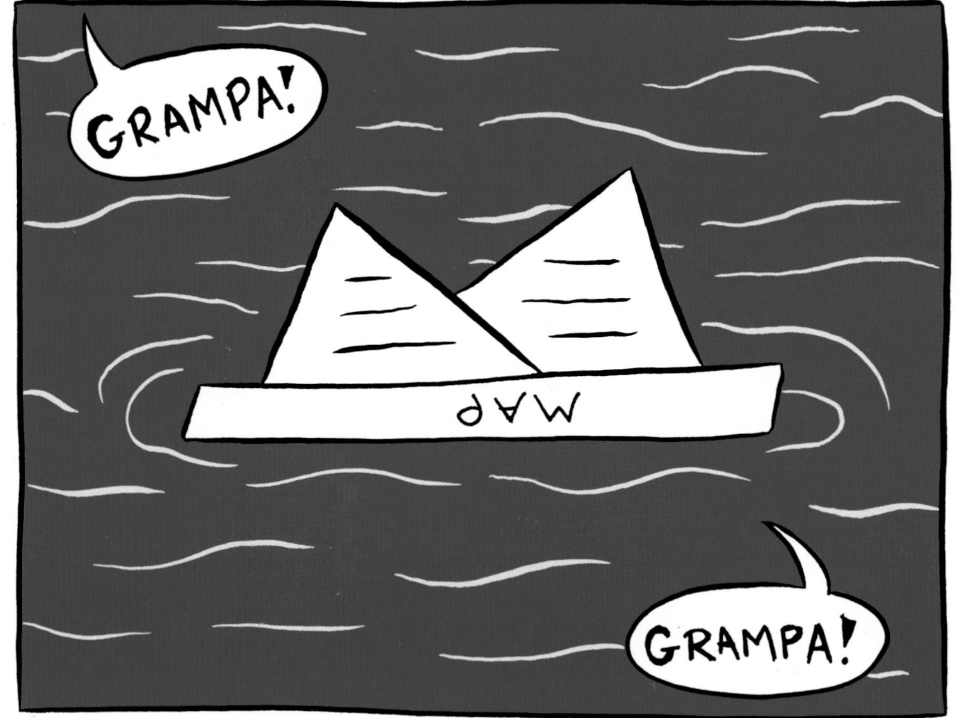
GRAMPA!
MAP
GRAMPA!

DON'T WORRY, GRAMPA. I'LL SAVE YOU!
RAP

GOOD LUCK, JULIE!
RAP

THAT'S THE **SECOND** WEIRDEST FISH I'VE EVER SEEN.
THERE GOES THE NEIGHBORHOOD.

?
SECRET UNDER WATER CAVE
(PLEASE WIPE FEET BEFORE ENTERING.)

GRAMPA?

OH, HI JULIE.

WHAT ARE YOU DOING HERE? WHY ARE YOU IN YOUR UNDERWEAR? AND WHO THE HECK ARE **THEY**?

DRIP.
WELL, MY CLOTHES GOT ALL WET, SO I TOOK THEM OFF.

AND WE'RE MONKEYS!
YEAH, MONKEYS!
OH, I GET IT. YOU'RE "SEA MONKEYS."

TECHNICALLY, SINCE WE'RE AT THE BOTTOM OF THE OCEAN, WE'RE OCEAN MONKEYS.
OH.

AND FOR YEARS WE'VE BEEN TRYING TO GET THE LID OFF OF THIS PEANUT BUTTER JAR.
PEANUT BUTTER

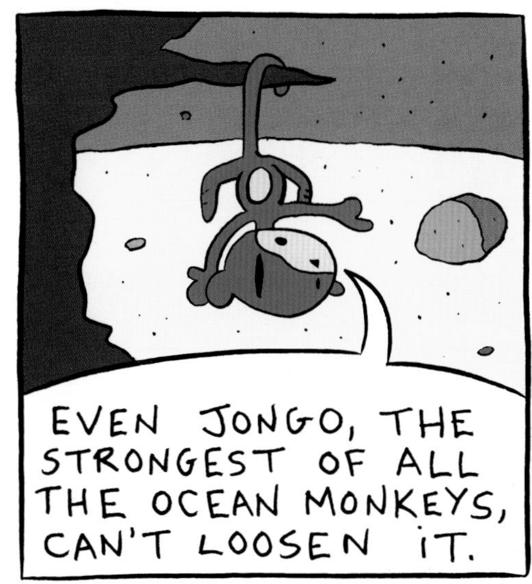
EVEN JONGO, THE STRONGEST OF ALL THE OCEAN MONKEYS, CAN'T LOOSEN IT.

IT'S REALLY STUCK ON TIGHTLY!
BODY BY KONG

JU-LIE!

JU-LIE!

YOU CAN DO IT!

JU-LIE!

HERE, LET ME TRY.
MAP
I'M SURE THAT A PERFECT HUMAN SPECIMEN LIKE MYSELF WILL HAVE NO TROUBLE OPENING IT.

THREE HOURS LATER...
Z Z Z
GRRRRR. THIS...THING ...WON'T... BUDGE.
MAP

ALL IS LOST! THIS IS TERRIBLE! WE'LL **NEVER** HAVE OUR PEANUT BUTTER. BUT I'M SO VERY HUNGRY...WOE IS ME!
JELLY
BREAD
NO, WAIT!

I KNOW WHAT TO DO!

GRAMMA TAUGHT ME THAT IF A LID IS STUCK, YOU CAN RUN IT UNDER HOT WATER...
HOT SPRING

THE HEAT WILL MAKE THE METAL EXPAND AND...

HOORAY!

OUR HERO!

POP!

PEANUT BUTTER

GOSH, YOU MUST HAVE MAGICAL POWERS.
WELL, ACTUALLY, IT'S JUST SCIENCE.

BECAUSE YOU'VE HELPED US, WE CROWN YOU KING OF THE OCEAN MONKEYS,
SQ

GOOEY FROOT
BUBBLE GUM
AND AWARD YOU THE SECRET OF THE GIANT SHARK.

I DON'T UNDERSTAND. THIS IS NO SECRET. IT'S JUST A REGULAR PACK OF CHEWING GUM.
SQ
JJW
MMM. TUTTI-FRUTTI! MY FAVORITE!

DON'T ASK US. IT'S A SECRET TO US, TOO.
MAP
CHOMP.
CHOMP.
OH, WELL. I GUESS WE SHOULD BE GOING.

THANKS AGAIN! WE'LL NEVER FORGET YOU!
MMM-HMM!

WELL, THEY SURE WERE NICE HUMANS.
YUP. HEY, LET'S OPEN OUR CAN OF BANANA JUICE TO CELEBRATE.
JUICE

BANANA JUICE
BANANA
SNAP
OOPS.

NOOOOO!
BANANA
AND SO IT GOES...

WHOEVER HEARD OF A SHARK THAT LIKES GUM? THAT'S CRAZY TALK.
I PREFER SALTWATER TAFFY MYSELF.

BACK ON THE SURFACE...
HEY, GRAMPA.
GASP

DIDN'T WE HAVE A BOAT UP HERE?
WE'RE DOOMED!

NO, LOOK! IT'S DJ CHICKEN AND MC SQUIRREL'S LIFE RAFT.

THEY LEFT US A NOTE!
MEMO
TO: GRAMPA
CC: JULIE
RE: YOUR BOAT
WE BORROWED IT!
SINCERELY,
DJ CHICKEN
MC SQUIRREL

GOSH, THOSE TWO SURE ARE POLITE.
UM, GRAMPA?

AND GOOD RAPPERS TOO. I REMEM—
GRAMPA!

JULIE, DON'T YOU KNOW IT'S RUDE TO INTER— OH. AHHHHHH!

IT'S STEPHEN, THE LARGEST SHARK IN THE WORLD, AND HE LOOKS HUNGRY! LET'S GET OUT OF HERE!
I'LL UNPLUG THE AIR VALVE.
FISSSS
GRAMPA, I DON'T THINK THAT'S THE BEST IDE-

AHH H HH!
PSSST

WHEE EEE!
PSSSST

PERHAPS THAT WASN'T EXACTLY THE SMARTEST THING TO DO.
GLUG
MAP
GLUG
OH WELL. IT'S BEEN NICE WORKING WITH YOU.

GRAMPA, DO YOU HAVE ANY OF THAT BUBBLE GUM LEFT?
MAP
YES, BUT IT'S MY LAST PIECE.

THIS IS NO TIME TO BE GREEDY!
GIVE IT TO STEPHEN, QUICKLY!

TREMBLE
MAP
TREMBLE

?
CHOMP
?
CHOMP

MWAHH!

PLUS, WE FINALLY GOT A CHANCE TO SEE HIM UP CLOSE AND PERSONAL.

UM, JULIE THIS MIGHT NOT BE THE BEST TIME TO BRING THIS UP...

BUT I **REALLY** HAVE TO GO TO THE BATHROOM.
OH, GRAMPA.
MMM... TUTTI-FRUTTI.

chapter two

SO THERE WE WERE IN THE MIDDLE OF THE OCEAN WITHOUT A BOAT OR FOOD. WE WERE EVEN OUT OF BUBBLE GUM!

Dear Gramma,
MAP

Having a great time. Wish you were here.
I GUESS "GREAT" IS A BIT OF AN EXAGGERATION. WE ARE STRANDED OUT HERE WITHOUT OUR SHIP. I JUST DON'T WANT HER TO WORRY.

HERE, MR. PELICAN. PLEASE DELIVER THIS TO MY GRAMMA.
MAP

NO! DON'T EAT IT!
GULP.

BURRP!
THIS IS HOPELESS.

OH, REALLY?
WE'RE SAVED!
BUT WHAT'S THAT ON THEIR FLAG?

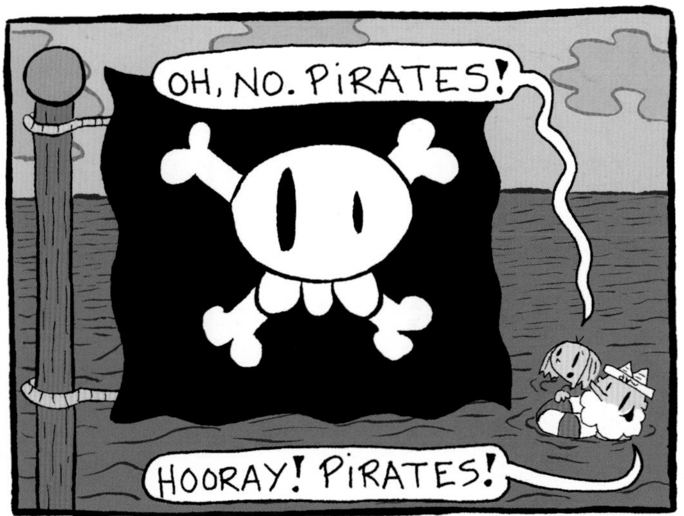
OH, NO. PIRATES!
HOORAY! PIRATES!

WELCOME ABOARD.
UM, NO OFFENSE, BUT YOU DON'T **LOOK** LIKE BLOODTHIRSTY CRIMINALS.
STOCKS
MAP
WELL, TO KEEP UP WITH THE TIMES, WE'VE HAD TO MAKE A FEW CHANGES.

FOR EXAMPLE, I USED TO WEAR AN EYE PATCH, BUT NOW I WEAR THESE SPIFFY TINTED GLASSES.

AND OUR WEBSITE GETS MORE THAN THIRTY HITS PER DAY!
TOMB RAVER
PIRATED SOFTWARE

ROLLERBLADES? GLASSES? WEBSITE? WHAT KIND OF STINKY PIRATES ARE YOU?
MAP
GRAMPA, SHHH.

MAP
WHY, I BET YOU'VE NEVER EVEN **HEARD** OF WALKING THE PLANK.
AND SO...

DID ANYONE EVER TELL YOU THAT YOU HAVE A BIG MOUTH?
MAP
YEAH, I GET THAT A LOT.
LESS TALKING, MORE WALKING.

WHAT A LOVELY DAY FOR A WALK.

AHHHH!
AHHHH!
IS THIS THE END OF OUR HEROES?

AHHHHHHH!
KER SPLASH!
I GUESS NOT.

WELCOME
FIRST ANNUAL
SHARK HUNTERS
CONVENTION
THIS WAY.
OH WELL.
HOW FORTUNATE.

PLEASE TAKE YOUR SEATS. THE CONVENTION IS ABOUT TO BEGIN.

fig. 1
GOOD AFTERNOON. WE ARE YOUR HOSTS, WILLIAM AND CLAUDIA.

PSST. HOW COME THERE AREN'T MORE PEOPLE HERE?
PROBABLY BECAUSE I FORGOT TO PUT THE AD IN **SHARKS ILLUSTRATED** MAGAZINE.

UM, IT'S GREAT TO SEE SO MANY SMILING FACES.
TODAY WE WILL DETERMINE WHICH TWO OF YOU WILL JOIN US ON OUR MISSION TO FIND STEPHEN, THE LARGEST SHARK IN THE WORLD.

WE WILL DO THIS BY MEANS OF THE MOST NOBLE OF COMPETITIONS...
CLAP
CLAP
A BAKE-OFF!

20 MINUTES AT 350° LATER...
HERE! TRY MY SPECIAL COOKIES...
MAP
PFFFT!
ASPARAGUS-PINEAPPLE SCOTCHIES!
ICK! BUT I GUESS SINCE YOU'RE THE ONLY CONTESTANT, YOU WIN!
MAP
#1 CHEF
WOW, WHAT AN HONOR. DO YOU WANT ANOTHER ONE?
NOOOO! ANYTHING BUT THAT!
LET'S GO FIND THE SHARK INSTEAD.

YOU DON'T PLAN ON HURTING STEPHEN, DO YOU?
William + Claudia BRAND CAT FOOD
soon with shark meat!
MAP
OF COURE NOT! WHAT WOULD GIVE YOU THAT CRAZY IDEA?

COME ON, GET iN!
UNTIE
UNTIE

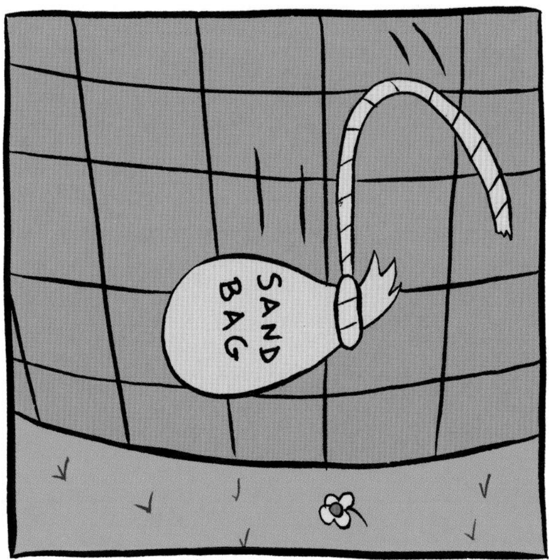
SAND BAG

WE'RE TAKING OFF!
STEPHEN THE SHARK HERE WE COME!
MAP
SAND BAG
SAND BAG
SAND BAG

TURN LEFT AT THE VOLCANO.
BLOOP
BLOOP

HANG A RIGHT AT THE TIDAL WAVE.

GO AROUND THE BOLTS OF LIGHTNING.
CAT FOOD

William + Claudia BRAND
CAT FOOD
MAKE A U-TURN AT THE THREE-HEADED MONSTER.

WELL, FOR STARTERS, WE'RE LOOKING FOR A SHARK IN THE MIDDLE OF THE DESERT.

William + Claudia BRAND CAT FOOD

OH, THAT.

DID SOMEONE SAY **DESSERT?** I'M **STARVING.**

THAT'S **DESERT,** GRAMPA.

LET'S LAND AND GET OUR BEARINGS.

SEE, I TOLD YOU WE SHOULD HAVE TURNED LEFT AT ALBUQUERQUE.
UM, JULIE?

NO, NO, NO. WE SHOULD HAVE HUNG A RIGHT AT HOBOKEN.
JULIE?
WHAT IS IT GRAMPA?

ZZZIP
OH, NOTHING.

WA...TER.
WA...TER.

DYING...OF...THIRST.
GRAMPA, CUT IT OUT! WE JUST LOST THE BALLOON FIVE MINUTES AGO.

BUT, JULIE, THIS IS RIDICULOUS. **EVERYONE** KNOWS THAT THE DESERT IS THE ABSOLUTE **WORST** PLACE TO LOOK FOR A SHARK.
NASA
H_2O
MAP

WHAT THE HECK IS STEPHEN DOING IN THE MIDDLE OF THE DESERT INSIDE OF A GIANT WATER-FILLED ROCKET SHIP?!

I DON'T KNOW. BUT LET'S SNEAK DOWN THERE AND FIND OUT!
MAP

AND SO...
HEY, JULIE, WANT A BITE OF MY SUPER-SOUR GIANT GUMMI OCTOPUS CANDY?
NASA
H_2O
Z Z Z Z
AW, COME ON!
KEEP OUT!
GRAMPA, BE QUIET OR YOU'LL WAKE THE GUARD.

NYAH NYAH.
MAP
Z Z Z

HOW DO YOU SUPPOSE STEPHEN GOT HERE?

IT LOOKS LIKE WHEN THEY WERE SUCKING UP WATER THEY ACCIDENTALLY GOT STEPHEN AS A BONUS.
TO OCEAN

COME ON. THERE MUST BE A RELEASE SWITCH AT THE TOP.

THEN WE CAN CAPTURE – I MEAN, THEN WE CAN **RELEASE** STEPHEN.
Z
Z
Chet

NOW DO YOU WANT SOME CANDY, JULIE?
NASA
H_2O
NO OFFENSE, GRAMPA, BUT IT SOUNDS GRODY.

BUT IT'S SO VERY, VERY YUMMY.
MAP
OOPS.

OH NO! IT'S GOING TO WAKE THE GUARD!
Z
Z
Z
ROCKET CON

WHEW. IT MISSED.
Z
Z
Z
Z

SEE, JULIE, I **KNEW** NOTHING WOULD...
ZZZZZ
ROCKET CONTROL
BOING

...HAPPEN.
CLICK.
LAUNCH BUTTON
LUNCH BUTTON

GRAMPA, PLEASE TELL ME THAT'S YOUR STOMACH RUMBLING.
BLOOP.
RUMBLE.
BLOOP.
RUMBLE.
PLOP.
WELL, I **AM** A BIT PECKISH.

RUMBLE
RUMBLE
HEY! COME BACK! YOU DON'T KNOW HOW TO FLY THAT THING!

WOO-HOO!

DON'T LET GO, CLAUDIA! REMEMBER WE NEED THE SHARK MEAT FOR OUR CAT FOOD COMPANY.
CAT FOOD?
SURE, WHAT DID YOU THINK?
THAT WE WERE GOING TO STUDY HIM? WE'RE CATS, FOR PETE'S SAKE!
BYE!
NO!
MAP
AHHHHH!

CATCH.

BUDDA
BUDDA

GRAMMA?
JULIE, HAVE YOU BEEN TAKING YOUR MULTIVITAMINS?
GET IN!

HOW DID YOU FIND US?
WELL, JULIE, IMAGINE MY SURPRISE WHEN I CRACKED OPEN AN EGG AND DISCOVERED A NOTE FROM MY FAVORITE GRANDAUGHTER.
BUDDA
BUDDA

BUT, GRAMMA, WHAT ARE WE GOING TO DO ABOUT STEPHEN?
DON'T WORRY, DEAR. WE'LL GET MY ROCKET.

YOU HAVE A ROCKET?!
OF COURSE. EVERY GRAMMA DOES. WE JUST DON'T BRAG ABOUT IT.

HOLD ON TO YOUR DENTURES!

MAP
BUDDA
BUDDA
BUDDA
BUDDA

UM, I THINK GRAMPA JUST BARFED IN HIS HAT.
BUDDA
BUDDA
OH, MERTON.

chapter three

SURE ENOUGH GRAMMA DID HAVE A ROCKET, SO OFF WE WENT INTO OUTER SPACE TO FIND STEPHEN. IT ALL SEEMED LIKE A DREAM TO ME.

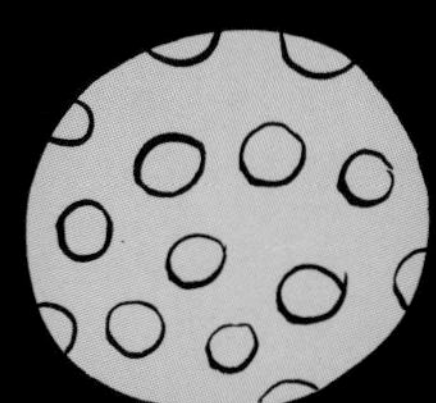

GRAMPA! GRAMPA!
WHAT IS IT, DEAR?

I JUST HAD THE WEIRDEST DREAM.
WE WERE ON A MISSION TO FIND STEPHEN AND THESE TWO MEAN CATS, WILLIAM AND CLAUDIA.

THEY WANTED TO TURN STEPHEN INTO CAT FOOD. AND THE ODDEST THING WAS THAT WE ENDED UP IN GRAMMA'S ROCKET IN SPACE.
LITTLE STEVIE
WOW.

THAT IS A WEIRD DREAM!
ATTENTION, MERTON AND JULIE!

INTERCOM
THIS IS GRAMMA! COME TO THE BRIDGE OF MY ROCKET IMMEDIATELY. I'VE LOCATED STEPHEN THE SHARK AND THOSE PESKY TALKING CATS. OH, AND I'M GOING TO TURN ON THE ARTIFICIAL GRAVITY NOW.

FLAP
MAP
UH-OH.
FLAP.

ZZIP!
THUD.

GET DRESSED, JULIE. LOOKS LIKE WE'VE GOT OURSELVES AN ADVENTURE.

ON THE BRIDGE...
MY CALCULATIONS INDICATE THAT STEPHEN IS ON THE PLANET PURPLE AND IS IN GREAT DANGER.
WE'VE GOT TO HELP HIM!

THAT'S WHY I'M SENDING YOU AND GRAMPA DOWN TO INVESTIGATE.
WHY AREN'T YOU COMING WITH US?
SHE PROBABLY HAS TO KNIT A SWEATER OR SOMETHING.

ACTUALLY, YOU OLD FOOL, I'M TRAINING FOR THE OLYMPICS.
GO GRAMMA!
ARE YOU SURE THAT'S WHERE STEPHEN THE SHARK IS?

OF COURSE! I'M ABSOLUTELY, POSITIVELY, 100 PERCENT SURE. NOW PUT ON YOUR SPACESUIT!
YES, DEAR.

ON PLANET PURPLE...
SPACE JORDANS
I'M TELLING YOU, JULIE, GRAMMA DOESN'T RESPECT ME.

I MEAN I **AM** THE MOST FAMOUS ICHTHYOLOGIST* IN THE WORLD!
MAP
(*AN ICHTHYOLOGIST IS A FISH SCIENTIST.)

I JUST WISH SOMEONE WOULD APPRECIATE ME.
!
OUR HERO

MAP
HURRY UP! YOU'RE JUST IN TIME FOR YOUR SPEECH.
SPEECH?

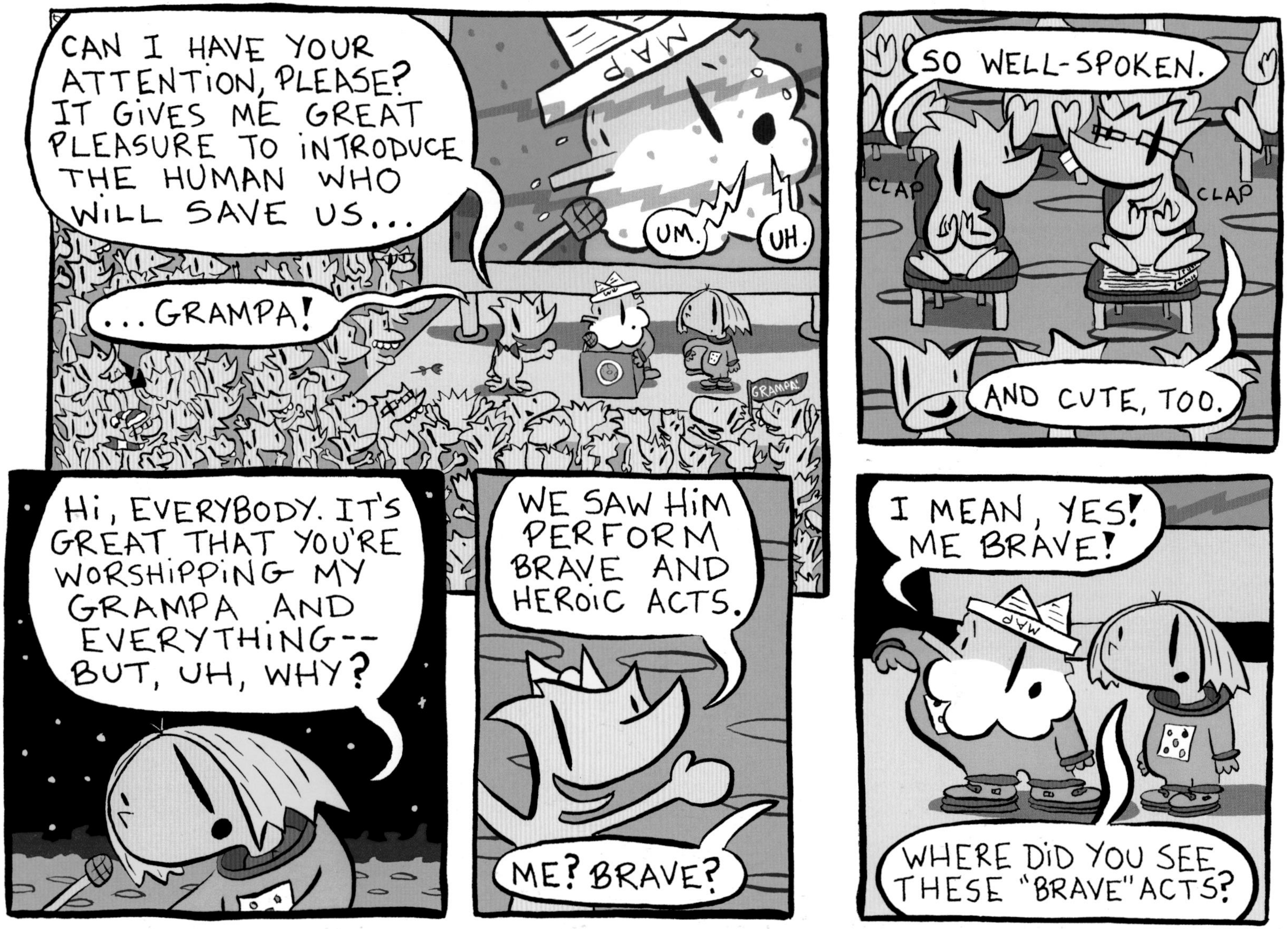

CAN I HAVE YOUR ATTENTION, PLEASE? IT GIVES ME GREAT PLEASURE TO INTRODUCE THE HUMAN WHO WILL SAVE US...

UM.

UH.

...GRAMPA!

Hi, EVERYBODY. IT'S GREAT THAT YOU'RE WORSHIPPING MY GRAMPA AND EVERYTHING-- BUT, UH, WHY?

WE SAW HIM PERFORM BRAVE AND HEROIC ACTS.

ME? BRAVE?

ON TV, OF COURSE.
MAP
CHOMP
NATURE CHANNEL
CLICK
OH. THEY SAID THEY WOULD EDIT THIS PART OUT.

WHY IS THE PICTURE SO FULL OF STATIC?
THAT'S WHY WE NEED YOUR HELP. JORDAN, THE EVIL SCIENTIST-MONSTER, MUST BE JAMMING THE SIGNAL.

SCIENTIST-MONSTER?
UM, FUNNY THING. I JUST REMEMBERED I'VE GOT A VERY IMPORTANT BARBER'S APPOINTMENT. BYE.

SNIFF
OH, DON'T LOOK AT US LIKE THAT.

WE UNDERSTAND. ›SNIFF‹ YOU'RE BUSY.
SNIFF
FINE! WE'LL VISIT THIS SCIENTIST-MONSTER. JUST QUIT FAKE-CRYING!

HUZZAH!
EVIL SCIENTIST-MONSTER.
BESIDES, MAYBE WE'LL FIND WHERE STEPHEN IS.

LATER...
HEY, THE RECEPTION JUST GOT BETTER!
THEY MUST HAVE DEFEATED JORDAN!

GUYS, I'M DONE WITH THE HAIR DRYER. SORRY IF THAT MESSED UP THE TELEVISION.

!
!
UH, WHAT'S WRONG?

I SURE HOPE THIS MONSTER'S GOT A BATHROOM. I REALLY HAVE TO GO.
DING DONG
GET LOST!

PLEASE, COME IN.

HA HA HA! (THAT'S DIABOLICAL LAUGHTER, BY THE WAY.) HA HA!
I'VE TAKEN THE LIBERTY OF TYING YOU TO MY LATEST INVENTION.

...MY BAKING-SODA-AND-VINEGAR BOMB.
UM, DON'T WE GET A LAST MEAL?

I GUESS THAT WOULD BE THE DECENT THING TO DO.
I THINK I'VE GOT SOME LEFTOVER CHINESE FOOD IN THE FRIDGE.

MMM. PRETTY GOOD, BUT IT NEEDS PEPPER.
SHAKE
SHAKE

AHH
...CHOO!

BLESS YOU.
WHAT DID YOU SAY?

UM, YOU SNEEZED, SO I SAID "BLESS YOU."
BWAHH!
SLURP
THAT'S THE NICEST THING ANYONE'S EVER SAID TO ME.

SNIFF. POLITENESS IS ALL TOO RARE THESE DAYS.
WOULD YOU CARE FOR A CUP OF HERBAL TEA?

TWO HOURS LATER...
Z Z Z
SIP
AND THIS IS ME AS DADDY WARBUCKS IN THE PURPLE PLANET COMMUNITY THEATRE'S PRODUCTION OF "ANNIE." YOU SEE, I'M JUST A SCIENTIST-MONSTER TO PAY THE RENT.

WELL, WE SHOULD BE GOING. THANKS FOR THE TEA AND THE CONVERSATION AND, MOST OF ALL, FOR DEACTIVATING THE BOMB.
Z Z Z
SHAKE
SHAKE

BEEP
BEEP
MAP
HEAD SHOTS
DEACTIVATING THE WHAT NOW?

0:03
BEEP.
0:02
BEEP.
0:01
BEEP.
BLOOP
MAP
BLOOP
0:00
ESCAPE POD.
RUMBLE
BLOOP
GLUG
UH-OH.

KABLAMMO!

AHHHHHH!
MAP

AHHH!

CRASH!

HOW FORTUNATE. WE LANDED IN OUR OWN SPACESHIP.
Hi, GRAMMA.

WELL, WELL, WELL. IF IT ISN'T MY TWO MOST FAVORITE PEOPLE IN THE UNIVERSE. YOU'RE JUST IN TIME.
TIME FOR WHAT?

TIME TO PLAY VIDEO GAMES?
TIME FOR ICE-CREAM SUNDAES?
MAP
SLURP
DUST
DUST
UH, NOT EXACTLY...

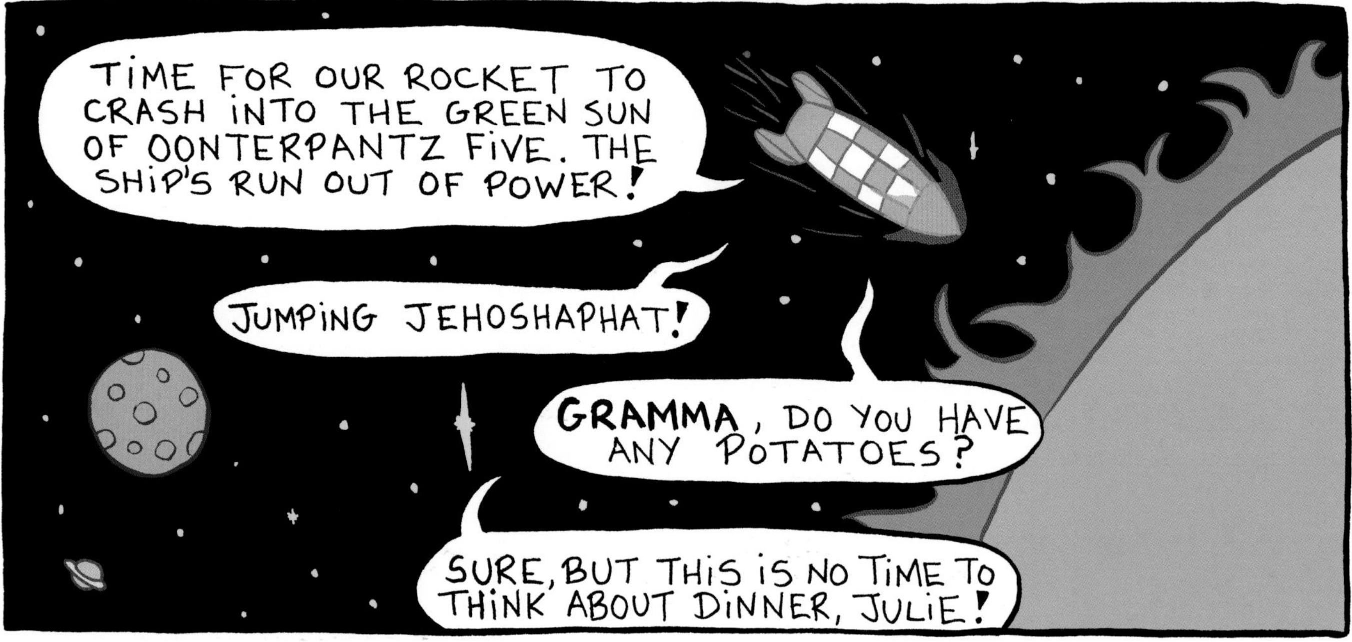
TIME FOR OUR ROCKET TO CRASH INTO THE GREEN SUN OF OONTERPANTZ FIVE. THE SHIP'S RUN OUT OF POWER!
JUMPING JEHOSHAPHAT!
GRAMMA, DO YOU HAVE ANY POTATOES?
SURE, BUT THIS IS NO TIME TO THINK ABOUT DINNER, JULIE!

YOU REALLY TAKE AFTER YOUR GRAMPA.
NO.

IN SCIENCE CLASS I LEARNED THAT WE CAN GENERATE ELECTRICITY WITH A POTATO.
ROCKET POWER

IT'S WORKING!
ZOOM!
HUZZAH!

BZZT. BZZT. BZZT.
NOW WHAT?
THE SHARKOMETER HAS LOCATED STEPHEN THE SHARK. HE'S ON PLANET FIESTA.

OH, NO. IS THERE SOMETHING WRONG WITH HIM?
MMN. MN.
NO. IT'S MUCH MORE URGENT! SENSORS INDICATE THAT IT'S STEPHEN'S BIRTHDAY!

AND HE'S HAVING A PARTY! **AND** WE'RE INVITED!
HAPPY BIRTHDAY
SET COURSE: PLANET FIESTA.
CLICK

DO YOU THINK THAT'S PLANET FIESTA?
I'VE GOT A FUNNY FEELING THAT IT IS.
I'LL LAND THE SHIP.
MAP

THERE'S THE PARTY!
FFT.
LOOKS LIKE WE'RE JUST IN TIME TO SING...

TO... YOU!
WELL, ALMOST.
YAY!

WOW, LOOK AT ALL THE COOL PRESENTS.
JAWS
HUNEY
ANTS
MAP
A WAFFLE IRON, A POLKA MUSIC CD, CROSS-COUNTRY SKIS, AN ANT FARM...

COME ON, GUYS. IT'S TIME FOR THE DANCE CONTEST.
DANCE CONTEST? THAT SOUNDS LIKE FUN!

OF COURSE, INTERGALACTIC LAW DICTATES THAT IF I, GRAG THE BOUNTY HUNTER, WIN, I GET TO MAKE STEPHEN MY SERVANT.

THAT'S NOT VERY NICE. WHO INVITED THIS GUY, ANYWAY?

AND HAVE I MENTIONED THAT I'M A WORLD-CLASS GROOVY DANCER?
GREAT. JUST GREAT.

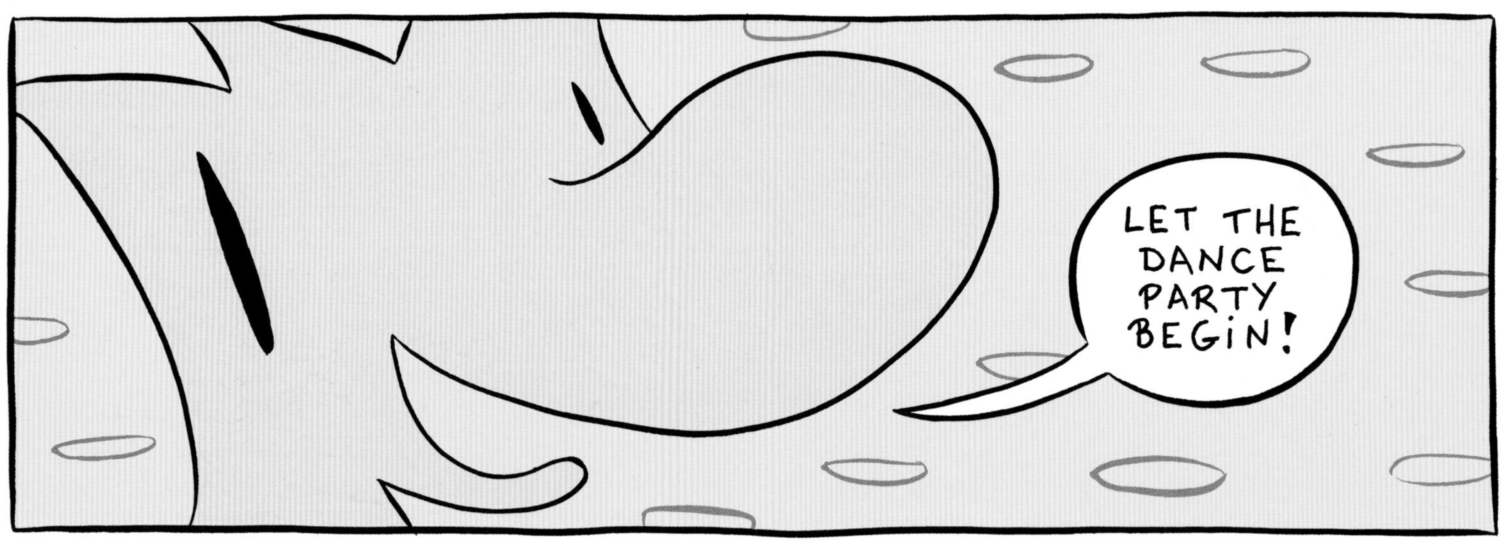
LET THE DANCE PARTY BEGIN!

RAP

SPIN

MEANWHILE...
ANTS
MILK
SO, YOU SEE, AT FIRST WE WANTED TO EAT STEPHEN...
BUT THEN WE LEARNED TO LOVE THE BIG GUY.
AND THE WINNER IS...
SCRATCH
SCRATCH
MILK

GRAG!
#1
GROOVY
WAIT A MINUTE. IT SEEMS WE HAVE A LAST-MINUTE ENTRY.

SCRATCH
SCRATCH
SCRATCH
SCRATCH
SCRATCH
ZIP
GOSH, THAT GUY'S GOT THE MOVES! IT ALMOST LOOKS AS IF HE'S GOT ANTS IN HIS PANTS. I THINK WE HAVE A NEW WINNER!

OH, MERTON, I'M SO PROUD OF YOU!
WHAT A PARTY! GRAMPA WON A TROPHY; GRAG'S HEADING BACK TO DANCING SCHOOL. WHAT MORE COULD HAPPEN?
mommy.

MOMMY?

chapter four

WE HAD FINALLY FOUND STEPHEN! BUT HE MISSED HIS MOMMY, SO GRAMPA AND I SET OUT TO FIND HER WHILE GRAMMA MONITORED OUR PROGRESS FROM HER HI-TECH LAB.

DON'T WORRY, STEPHEN. I'M SURE GRAMPA IS HARD AT WORK TRYING TO FIND YOUR MOMMY.
COME ON, GRAMPA! THIS IS NO TIME FOR MAKING SNOW ANGELS. GRAMMA SAID THAT WE ARE NEAR THE LAST KNOWN LOCATION OF STEPHEN THE SHARK'S MOTHER.

I SURE HOPE WE SEE LOTS OF PENGUINS. THEY'RE SO CUTE!
SPLAT.
OUCH.
GRAMPA, EVERYONE KNOWS THERE ARE NO PENGUINS AT THE NORTH POLE...

...ONLY IN ANTARCTICA.
Penguins only live south of the Equator (and they don't wear glasses, silly).
SEE, IT SAYS SO IN MY BIRDWATCHING BOOK.

!
ONE, PLEASE.
Lemonade

SHAKE.
SHAKE.
WHAT THE HECK ARE YOU DOING IN THE ARCTIC?

OWNING AND OPERATING A LEMONADE STAND, OF COURSE.
THUD.
HOW'S BUSINESS?

NOT SO GOOD. NO ONE WANTS LEMONADE BECAUSE IT'S SO COLD OUT!
LEMONADE
I KNOW WHAT TO DO!

SOON...
HOT TAMALES!
EXTRA SPICY
GRAMPA, I DON'T SEE HOW GIVING AWAY FREE FOOD IS GOING TO HELP.

TRUST ME.
MUNCH.
MUNCH.

WA-TER!
WA-TER!

YOU SAVED MY BUSINESS!
AHHH!
HOW CAN I EVER THANK YOU?
Lemonade
Lemons

DO YOU KNOW WHERE WE COULD FIND THE MOM OF STEPHEN THE SHARK?
NO.

BUT I KNOW SOMEONE WHO DOES: THE SNOW QUEEN! SHE KNOWS WHERE EVERYONE IS. SHE'S MAGIC!
LEMON JUICE
Lemons
LET ME WRITE DOWN HOW TO CONTACT HER.

MAP
BUT THERE'S NOTHING ON THIS PAPER!

JULIE, I DON'T UNDERSTAND. WHY ARE YOU HOLDING MY READING GLASSES UP TO THE PAPER? I CAN'T SEE ANYTHING!
WATCH CAREFULLY.

THE MAGNIFIED HEAT FROM THE SUN MAKES THE LEMON JUICE VISIBLE.
GOOD WORK, JULIE! NOW WE'LL FIGURE OUT HOW TO SUMMON THE MYSTERIOUS SNOW QUEEN.

"1 CUP SUGAR. 2 TSP VANILLA."
IT'S A SECRET CODE!
NO, SILLY. IT'S A RECIPE FOR CHOCOLATE CAKE.
NOW LET'S GET COOKING!

20 MINUTES AT 425° LATER..
THE CAKE'S DONE. NOW WHAT?
PORTO STOVE
THE DIRECTIONS SAY TO GIVE YOUR WONDERFUL GRAMPA A BIG SLICE!

THEY DO NOT! GIVE ME THAT!
QUIT PULLING!
POOF!
HEY! STOP FIGHTING!

WHO DARES TO SUMMON THE ALL-KNOWING SNOW QUEEN!
UH, ME AND MY GRAMPA.
SAY, IS THAT CHOCOLATE CAKE I SMELL?

SOON...
YOUR HIGHNESS, NOW THAT YOU'VE FINISHED THE CAKE, WILL YOU REVEAL TO US THE LOCATION OF STEPHEN'S MOM?
BRRAP.
PAT. PAT.
LICK LICK.
YEAH, SURE THING, KID.

DO YOU HAVE ANY ANTACIDS, KID?
THE SNOW QUEEN'S GUT ISN'T WHAT IT USED TO BE.

ALL RIGHT. WHERE WAS I?
ZOOM
OH YEAH.

IN ORDER TO FIND STEPHEN'S MOM...
...YOU MUST EMBARK UPON A PERILOUS JOURNEY.
SQ
ACROSS THE SEA OF JELLO,
BOING.
FLOAT
FLOAT
OVER THE MOUNTAIN OF LIMBURGER CHEESE,
THROUGH THE RAIN OF THE BRUSSELS SPROUTS,
BENEATH THE VALLEY OF THE BUBBLE BATHS.
SCRUB.
SCRUB
GOSH.
YUCK.

NO, I'M AFRAID NOT. YOU MUST ENDURE THESE TESTS AND MORE. TESTS THAT WILL TAKE **YEARS** TO COMPLETE AND CHALLENGE THE LIMITS OF YOUR BRAVERY. ONLY **THEN** MAY YOU FIND STEPHEN'S MOM!

STEPHEN, GOOD NEWS! GRAMPA AND JULIE HAVE FOUND YOUR MOMMY IN THE ARCTIC! YOU'RE GIGANTIC; I BET YOUR MOM'S EVEN BIGGER!
YOU KNOW, I ALWAYS PICTURED YOU AS BEING...
...LESS TEENSY.
WHAT CAN I SAY? I GUESS HE GETS HIS SIZE FROM HIS DAD.
CHILDBIRTH WAS NO FUN, LET ME TELL YOU.
STEPHANIE, WHY DID YOU ABANDON STEPHEN WHEN HE WAS SUCH A YOUNG SHARK?
ME?! IT WAS HE THAT RAN AWAY.

"I REMEMBER IT AS THOUGH IT WERE YESTERDAY. YOUNG STEPHEN AND I WERE LOOKING FOR FOOD."
BRACES!
NO DESSERT UNTIL YOU'VE EATEN YOUR KRILL.
"WE CAME UPON A BOAT."
MERTON, STOP FOOLING AROUND!
THAT WAS GRAMPA WHEN HE WAS A BABY!
"THE SMALL CHILD SLIPPED AND FELL INTO THE OCEAN."
SLIP.
CHECK OUT THIS CONCENTRATION OF ALGAE!
OOO.
"I ALWAYS TAUGHT STEPHEN TO STAY AWAY FROM HUMANS. BUT HE DIDN'T LISTEN TO ME."

"HE RESCUED THE CHILD AND PUT HIM BACK ON THE BOAT. I DON'T THINK THE PARENTS EVEN NOTICED."
NO, HONEY. IT'S A POINT FOUR CONCENTRATION.

"GRAMPA GAVE STEPHEN SOME TUTTI-FRUTTI GUM TO THANK HIM."
IT'S ALL COMING BACK TO ME NOW!

"THE BOAT SAILED AWAY."
LET'S GO, STEPHEN. **NOW!**
"THAT NIGHT, STEPHEN SWAM AWAY TO FIND THE BOY AND MORE OF HIS DELICIOUS GUM."

AND THAT WAS THE LAST I SAW OF MY LITTLE BOY.
SNIFF
WOW, WHAT A STORY! BUT WHY ARE YOU IN THE ARCTIC?

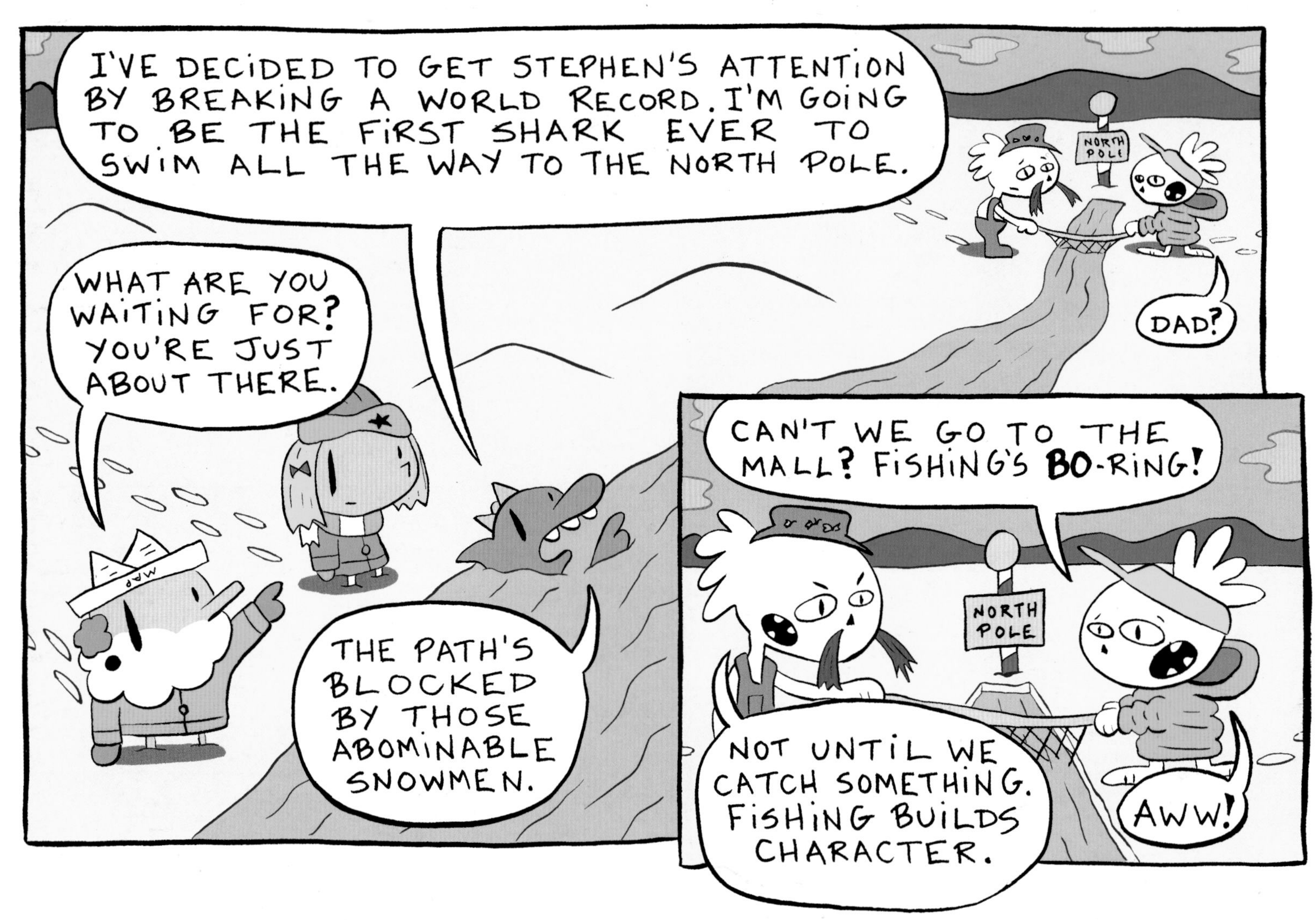
I'VE DECIDED TO GET STEPHEN'S ATTENTION BY BREAKING A WORLD RECORD. I'M GOING TO BE THE FIRST SHARK EVER TO SWIM ALL THE WAY TO THE NORTH POLE.
WHAT ARE YOU WAITING FOR? YOU'RE JUST ABOUT THERE.
THE PATH'S BLOCKED BY THOSE ABOMINABLE SNOWMEN.
NORTH POLE
DAD?
MAP
CAN'T WE GO TO THE MALL? FISHING'S BO-RING!
NORTH POLE
NOT UNTIL WE CATCH SOMETHING. FISHING BUILDS CHARACTER.
AWW!

BUT THEY'RE HAVING A SALE ON VISORS!
WE AGREED THAT TODAY WOULD BE A FATHER-SON BONDING DAY. SO START BONDING!

HMM.
UNSCREW.
SCREW.
A-HA!
SOON...
WELL, WELL, WELL! IF IT ISN'T MY LONG-LOST COUSINS.
NORTH POLE
HEY, WHAT SAY YOU LET US, I MEAN ME, HOLD THE NET FOR A WHILE.
(OUCH! GRAMPA, YOU'RE STEPPING ON MY HAIR.)
GRAMPA!
THE ZIPPER!
OOPS.
HEH-HEH.
FLOP.
AHH! PEOPLE!
THEY'RE SO WEIRD-LOOKING!
AND FURLESS!

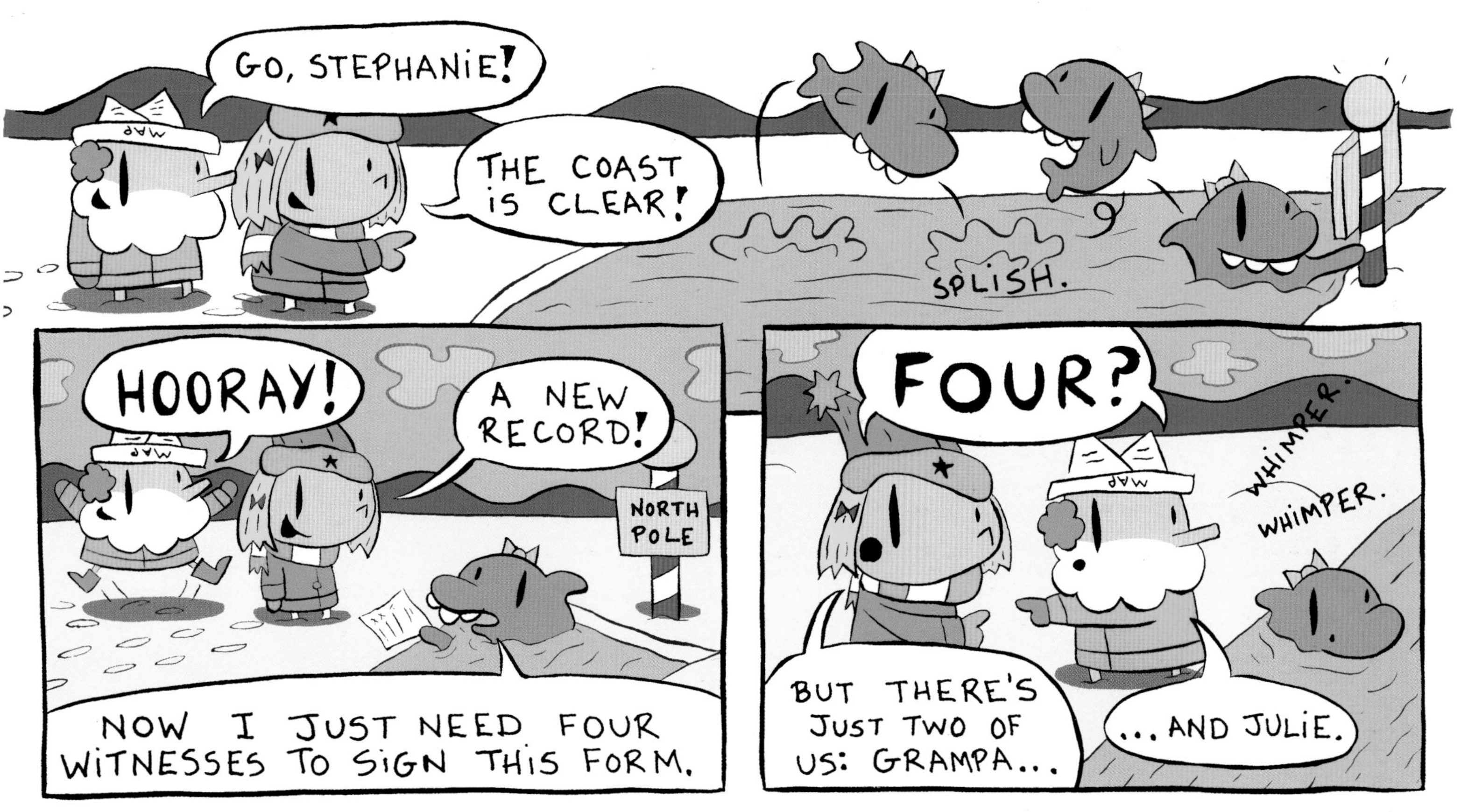
GO, STEPHANIE!
THE COAST IS CLEAR!
SPLISH.
NORTH POLE
HOORAY!
A NEW RECORD!
NOW I JUST NEED FOUR WITNESSES TO SIGN THIS FORM.
FOUR?
WHIMPER.
WHIMPER.
BUT THERE'S JUST TWO OF US: GRAMPA...
...AND JULIE.

PLEASE DON'T HURT US.
JUMP
WE'RE JUST POOR, DEFENSELESS ABOMINABLE SNOWMEN.

WE DON'T WANT TO HURT YOU. WE JUST NEED YOUR SIGNATURES ON THIS FORM.
SIGNATURES?
THEY WANT OUR AUTOGRAPHS!

"TO OUR BIGGEST FANS..."
UM, IT'S NOT REALLY AN AUTOGR-
GRAMPA, SHHH.

HOORAY (AGAIN)! WE'VE COMPLETED THE NECESSARY FORMS.
PUTT.
PUTT.
AND LOOK, STEPHANIE! HERE COMES GRAMMA IN HER HELICOPTER WITH YOUR LONG-LOST SON, STEPHEN!

OH, STEPHEN, I'VE MISSED YOU SO!
MAP
PUTT
PUTT
PUTT
PUTT
MAP
UH-OH.

PARDON ME, MR. WHALE, BUT IT SEEMS THAT YOU HAVE EATEN MY SON.
AND MY GRAMMA!
ME THOUGHT THEY WAS GRILLED CHEESE.

HOW ARE WE GOING TO GET THEM OUT?
I KNOW!

CLIMB.
CLIMB.
I'LL JUMP IN THE BLOWHOLE AND FIND GRAMMA AND STEPHEN...

THEN YOU MAKE THE WHALE LAUGH AND WE'LL ESCAPE THROUGH HIS MOUTH.

PLOOP.

SOON...
GOOD EVENING, LADIES AND GERMS.

WHERE DO FISH BUY THEIR SUPERHERO COSTUMES?

CAPE COD!
GET IT?

BA-DUM

TOUGH CROWD.

TWO HOURS LATER...
PROPS
WHOOP EEE
I'VE TRIED MY BEST MATERIAL AND NOT EVEN A GRIN.

NOTHING CAN MAKE THIS WHALE LAUGH.
WHOOP EEE
HUH, HUH. ME SEE HIS UNDERPANTS.

HA!
HA!
HA!
HA!

OH, STEPHEN I MISSED YOU SO VERY MUCH.
mommy.
GRAMPA, YOU DID IT! YOU MUST HAVE TOLD SOME HILARIOUS JOKES!
LET'S JUST SAY I LET IT ALL HANG OUT.

GET IT?
TOUGH CROWD.

THIS **BRUTE** ATE MY HELI-COPTER.

ME IS SORRY.

SEPTEMBER
AND TOMORROW'S THE FIRST DAY OF SCHOOL!

DON'T WORRY. I KNOW WHAT TO DO!

EXCUSE ME, STEPHEN, MAY I ASK A FAVOR OF YOU?

WHISPER
WHISPER
MAP

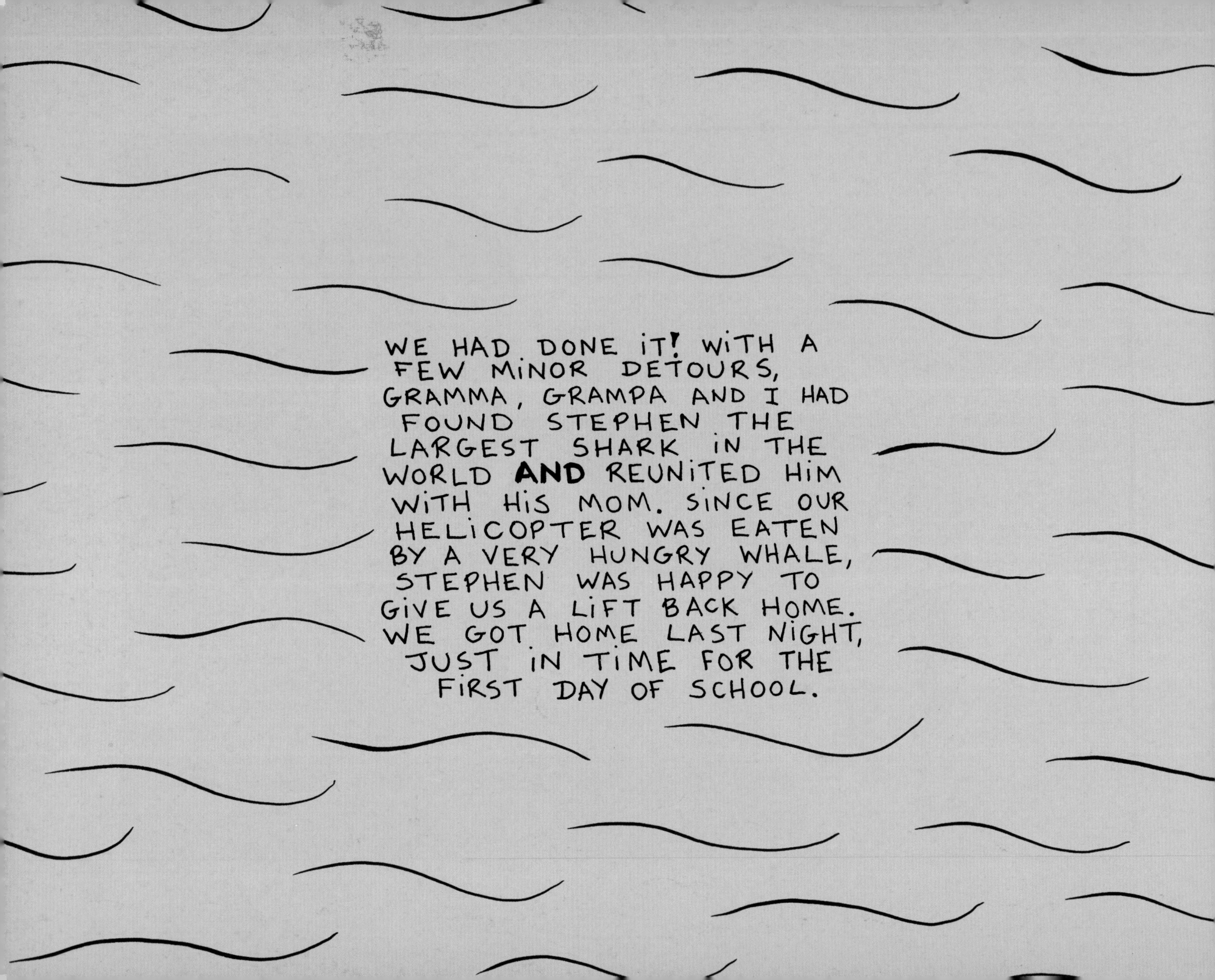
WE HAD DONE IT! WITH A FEW MINOR DETOURS, GRAMMA, GRAMPA AND I HAD FOUND STEPHEN THE LARGEST SHARK IN THE WORLD **AND** REUNITED HIM WITH HIS MOM. SINCE OUR HELICOPTER WAS EATEN BY A VERY HUNGRY WHALE, STEPHEN WAS HAPPY TO GIVE US A LIFT BACK HOME. WE GOT HOME LAST NIGHT, JUST IN TIME FOR THE FIRST DAY OF SCHOOL.

WE GOT HOME LAST NIGHT, JUST IN TIME FOR THE FIRST DAY OF SCHOOL.

OUR ART

AND THAT'S WHAT I DID...

ON...

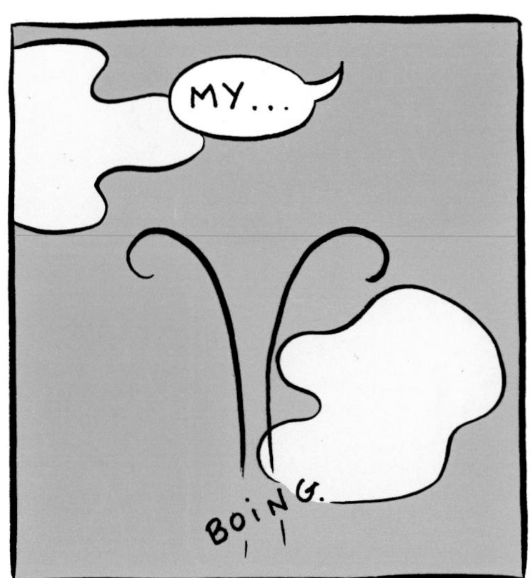
MY...
BOING.

SUMMER...
BOING

HI JULIE!
VACA-

JULIE, STOP STARING OUT THE WINDOW. YOU'RE NOT EVEN PAYING ATTENTION TO YOUR **OWN** REPORT.

I'M SORRY, MS. COOPER. IT'S JUST THAT I THOUGHT I SAW MY GRAMPA.

YOU'VE GOT QUITE THE ACTIVE IMAGINATION, YOUNG LADY.
2
+2
5
6
-1
8

FIRST, YOU MAKE UP ALL OF THOSE STORIES ABOUT YOUR SUMMER.
2
+2
5
6
-1
8

ABC
BONK
AND NOW YOU IMAGINE YOU SEE YOUR GRAMPA...

FLYING?
ABC
2
+2
5
6
-1
8

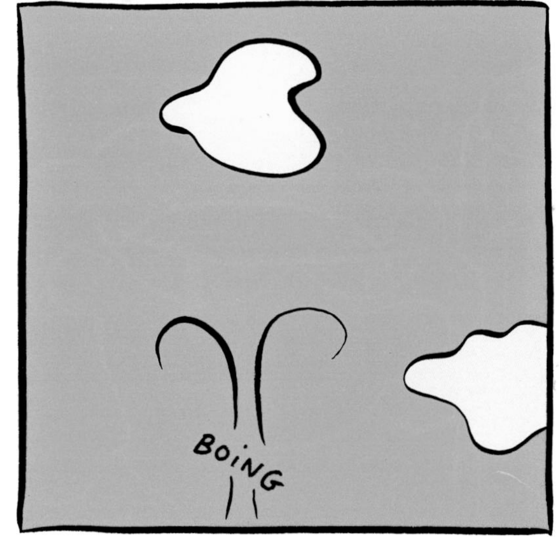

BOING

PORTO-TRAMPOLINE

GOOD DAY, SIR.
MAP
UH-OH.

AND SO...
PRINCIPAL'S OFFICE
NO WHINING
I DIDN'T KNOW THEY WERE EVEN **ALLOWED** TO SEND **GROWN-UPS** TO THE PRINCIPAL'S OFFICE!
WELL, GRAMPA, I HOPE YOU LEARNED YOUR LESSON.

YOU'VE GOT TO STOP GOOFING AROUND SO MUCH. IT'S TIME TO BUCKLE DOWN. LET'S SEE. WE'LL START TOMORROW MORNING AT 5 A.M. THE FIRST THING WE'LL SCHEDULE IS-
PRINCIPAL'S OFFICE
NO WHINING
DAILY PLANNER

GRAMPA?
PRINCIPAL'S OFFICE
NO WHINING

THUD
OW.

COME ON, JULIE! THERE'S LOTS MORE ADVENTURES TO BE HAD!
MAP

GRAMPA!

GET BACK IN HERE BEFORE WE GET IN **MORE** TROUBLE.

GRAMPA!

GRAMPA?
SiGH.

WAIT UP!
MAP

The End

this book is for shannon + summer + jennifer.

Jef Czekaj is a cartoonist, musician, and poster artist who lives and works in Somerville, Massachusetts. He is the co-founder of the Somerville Comics Collaborative, an organization dedicated to bringing people of all ages and backgrounds together around the common ground of storytelling using words and pictures. He is also a founding member of the Handstand Command, a Somerville-based music collective.

"Grampa and Julie: Shark Hunters" appears somewhat regularly in *Nickelodeon Magazine*. This is the first collection of their adventures.

Thanks: Jen Godfrey, Jordan Crane, Tom Devlin, James Kochalka, Dan Moynihan, Craig Bostick, Chris Staros and Brett Warnock at Top Shelf, the Xeric Foundation, William Braine, Claudia Depkin, Stephanie Melikian, Heath Row, the staff of *Nickelodeon Magazine* including Dave Roman, Carmen Morais, Catherine Tutrone, Hally Burak, and Laura Galen, the Diesel Café, the Czekajs, the Christensens, the Koniors, and the Godfreys.

Special thanks to Mr. Chris Duffy who helped shape these stories and is the best.